AHOY SAILOR!

AHOY SAILOR!
DANIEL ROZENSZTROCH

PHOTOGRAPHS
FRANCIS AMIAND

TEXT
CATHIE FIDLER

TRANSLATION FROM THE FRENCH
LAURENCE LECLERC

POINTED LEAF PRESS

CONTENTS

ALL ABOUT SAILORS, SEAMEN, AND THE WHOLE SHEBANG 16

THE SAILOR COLLECTED 24

THE CUTE LITTLE SAILOR 64

THE SAILOR IN LOVE 100

THE SAILOR AT WORK AT SEA 110

THE SAILOR AS MUSICIAN 136

THE SAILOR AS ARTIST AND MODEL 150

THE CELEBRITY SAILOR 160

THE SAILOR AT HOME 168

THE HEROIC SAILOR 180

THE SEXY SAILOR 200

ACKNOWLEDGMENTS AND INDEX 231

CAPTIONS AND PHOTOGRAPHY CREDITS 232

ALL ABOUT SAILORS, SEAMEN, AND THE WHOLE SHEBANG

Before diving into this book, let's try to define who the sailor, our titular character, really is. The poor sailor, barely a rung above ship's boy in naval hierarchy, must perform the lowliest duties on board. In the popular French nursery rhyme, "Il était un petit navire," or "Once upon a time, there was a small ship," a young sailor narrowly escapes being cooked and devoured by his starving older crewmates.

That being said, he's also the youngest and most attractive crew member: powerful yet delicate, both intimate and distant, evoking far horizons yet so very down to earth. He is, of course, immediately identified by his iconic attire. Sailors, seamen, salts, and tars commonly tickle the imagination of landlubbers, inhabiting a rich tapestry of daydreams and fantasies.

What is a sailor to avid collector Daniel Rozensztroch but a little guy setting off to explore the seven seas in his sexy uniform, among a group of other manly companions, coming ashore from time to time for a possibly steamy stopover?

Another burning question arises: why would Rozensztroch, after creating so many works centered on his collections, want to publish a book about sailors? This latest volume clearly shows our author has moved on to an addiction very different from its many previous iterations, which were all focused on everyday objects, all inanimate by nature. This time, the focus is undeniably human—fantasies included. Its representations in merchandise are countless, opening the floodgates to a new collection. Rozensztroch was initially attracted to folk-art images depicting sailors, but very soon, the seaman returned to shore, represented in the shape of everyday objects—a wonderfully and, as we will find out, incredibly varied group.

Our compulsive collector was seduced: he started seeing connections and linking the objects and images of his subject, weaving an intricate web that was both the cause and the consequence of his passion. This collection has led its author to reveal an intimate aspect that he'd never yet acknowledged. We could call it an assertive and avowed coming out of sorts!

But let's start by examining the symbolism of the theme. Why is the sailor such an attractive subject and why has he, throughout the ages, sparked such varied fantasies?

The character of the sailor appeals to children from an early age because of his weakness. He is vulnerable to the whims of nature as well as to those of his peers, who are dying to eat him up in every possible way. Another fascinating aspect of the sailor's character is that, snatched from such innocence, he is forced to toughen up at sea. This ordeal is admirable and terrifying to the rest of us. Imagine being kidnapped, also known as being shanghaied, from a bar—under-staffed captains were known to have unconscious drunken men abducted from taverns to make up the numbers in their crews. They would then set sail, and the victims would come to at sea and be made to toil for months. When at last they were released, they returned home with strong sea legs and a new virility.

The mariner is in fact a fearless adventurer, faced with the most perilous element: the sea itself. He elicits admiration and is undeniably erotic. He is the stuff of fantasies, endowed with youth, an impeccable physique and style, and an overt manliness that is enhanced by his fitted, easily shed bell-bottomed broadfall trousers and, of course, his "bad boy" reputation.

OPPOSITE Author and collector Daniel Rozensztroch's impressive private library is a testament to his interest and obsession with the worlds of design, crafts, and folk art.

Sailors were emblematic figures of male prostitution in the 19th century, as underpaid seamen were propositioned in every port by men and women alike. They inevitably succumbed and were tempted to offer up or willingly sell their services. One of the chapters in this book is devoted to photographs that so flagrantly display their subjects' virility that they must have been traded under the table.

In addition to the iconic bell-bottoms, other items of sailors' attire are highly seductive: their caps, known as *bachi* in the French Navy, are adorned with a red pompom, and touching it is believed to bring good luck. The same could be said of the oversized square "flap" collar for the navies in the United States and United Kingdom. The shoulder-borne sailor's duffel bag has been an endless inspiration for chic luggage makers and fashion designers—the most famous being Jean-Paul Gaultier—who have been reinterpreting the (obviously) navy blue pea jacket since the 1950s. A form-fitting shirt adorned with 21 horizontal stripes, reminiscent of the prison garb designed to insure fugitives were easily identified, completes the look Gaultier glorified in his 1984 "Boy Toy" collection.

All this leads to a thriving array of popular iconography. We will come across multifaceted images of our little hero throughout these pages, which include a variety of vintage photographs—souvenir pictures and portraits taken by local photographers; artworks in widely differing styles; communication tools, such as postage stamps and postcards; illustrations—sketches, etchings, pastels, posters, and advertisements. Each image depicts the main character and his milieu, as well as the fantasy figure he evokes, especially in the collection of highly erotic pictures. And the erotic portrayals are for the most part photographs.

But these two-dimensional representations of the sailor could not satisfy our obsessive collector. He needed more! So his collection was soon enriched with innumerable three-dimensional objects. In flea markets and online, the world teemed with everyday items representing our title character. He was figured in a variety of styles and materials attesting to the creativity and craftsmanship of his makers, offering Rozensztroch a fascinating cosmos that led him, with passion, down a rabbit hole of frenetic research.

Could this collection possibly be linked to his childhood? Are these images and effigies the playthings of an adult recalling his younger self? In a previous book, we learned that the author had spent many summers on the beaches of Scheveningen, near The Hague, a Dutch port presumably swarming with sailors of every kind. Another regular holiday destination for his family was Cannes, in the South of France, where the Sixth Fleet dropped anchor when it stopped in the Mediterranean. Sailors populated the bars at night, and were part of the scenery by day. The locals and tourists alike met them at every turn, often while being chased by the Naval Police, who were concerned with keeping the peace and protecting the image of the United States Navy.

Rozensztroch holds the Mediterranean dear to his heart, as he does other oceans and bodies of water. Enthusiastic for aquatic adventures and long-haul journeys, he's never been queasy or seasick on board, as his selection of objects, equally whimsical and uncompromising, reflects.

OPPOSITE Found in a flea market in Romania, this Tramp Art frame, made from small, cut pieces of wood, is a fitting enhancement to a photograph of a handsome sailor.

The photographs in this book shouldn't come as a surprise. The sailor's form—fashioned out of countless materials including ceramics, wood, bone, Bakelite, metal, and plastic—was often crafted by the seamen themselves, who used anything they had at hand during their rare moments of leisure. The sailor's image often embellished everyday objects—corkscrews, plates, glasses, bottles, ceramic cookie jars, and ashtrays.

Sailors are also notably represented on bowling pins and toys, made by the Radiguet company, among others. They also pop up in the form of rubber squeeze toys, characterized by the sharp squeal they produce when pressed. Toys inspired by our subject include the iconic Popeye the Sailor Man and Donald Duck in a sailor suit. Any good lead soldier collection holds a few sailors, and Duplo and Playmobil toys have recently adopted an unsurprisingly gender-neutral mariner. The Belgian cartoonist Georges Remi, who wrote under the pen name Hergé, featured a sailor in his comic series *The Adventures of Tintin*: Captain Archibald Haddock, albeit a retired captain, is invariably represented in his master mariner's uniform, with its distinctive cap and anchor-decorated sweater. Historically, every port on the globe offered kitschy sailor-themed souvenirs, and these figurines remain ubiquitous today.

Myriad superstitions arose from the many perils a sailor's life entailed. His character graces ex-votos and other votive offerings, and ornamental sailor figures were even seen to decorate marine-inspired Christmas nativity scenes, as the seaman and his family were in dire need of a saving faith.

The Greek artist Yannis Tsarouchis was also a rich source of inspiration to "marinophiles"— homophiles—as the clothed and unclothed sailors from his painting *The Forgotten Guard* allowed their fantasies to run free.

Jean Cocteau, the multitalented French poet, playwright, novelist, designer, filmmaker, and visual artist, who was a leader of the surrealist, avant-garde, and Dadaist movements, illustrated eloquent fantasies for the French novelist Jean Genet's *Querelle de Brest* of 1947. The very limited 460-copy print run of that work gives pride of place to the homosexuality of its hero—Jo, a.k.a. Querelle, is a young thug who manipulates and then murders his victims. Rozensztroch was lucky enough to secure a volume from a rare book dealer. A few pages can be seen here in an uncensored chapter, for admirers of the male physique. These images will reveal a very different aspect of the nautical mystique, the dark side of this collection, and bring to light the collector's inner secrets.

As we near the shore, we'll see how the author, in this amazing book, declares an avowed balance, a form of closure, even though we know his collector's compulsive thirst is never quenched. Bets are on for the subject of Rozensztroch's next obsession. In the meantime, anyone perusing these pages will delight in what he has captured in his nets and savor the salty flavor of his collection.

OPPOSITE In the tradition of Outsider Art, a wire object with a doll's glass eyes seems to direct its gaze toward an erotic photograph of a naked sailor. OVERLEAF An anonymous painting, found in a flea market, portrays a sailor in a ship's machine room.

Some collectors hoard their treasures in boxes, drawers, and closets, allowing them an occasional airing to be admired or to show them off to a few privileged enthusiasts—a far cry from Daniel Rozensztroch's philosophy: He has chosen to live with the objects he collects. Staged to complement each other, sailors are found throughout his home. A few examples of his organized hodgepodge include silver ex-votos, lead sailors, framed photographs, small paintings, figurines, and even bandanas. All this is beautifully presented and curated with the vision of a true stylist.

THE SAILOR COLLECTED

OPPOSITE Cookies kept inside this one-eyed sailor cookie jar in the kitchen of Daniel Rozensztroch's Paris loft will last as long as they do at sea.

OVERLEAF LEFT In the living room, a few scallop shells are cleverly decorated and arranged to commemorate a French sailor's visit to the port town of Marseille.

OVERLEAF RIGHT Three sailors are caught in a moment of hilarity in an ink drawing by an unknown artist. The drowsy sailor lying at the edge of the author's bookcase is hardly paying attention to them.

PAGE 28 The collector's paradox—contrasting a sculpted wooden sailor figurine with large hands and a polychromatic 17th-century sculpted wooden Virgin Mary who misplaced hers.

PAGE 29 The red pompom is the trademark of the French sailor's hat. This one is represented in a gouache of a proud sailor leaning against the bookshelves.

PAGE 30 Assorted objects surround a child's mask from the 1950s.

PAGE 31 Amorous messages from sailors peek out from romantic postcards placed in four Art Nouveau-style polychrome tole frames.

PAGE 32 A mix of romantic and humoristic vintage photographs and postcards have been affixed with magnets on a giant metal advertising letter.

PAGE 33 Top right, the long rectangular hand-colored gouache print is by George de Vertury, who was made the "official" painter for the French merchant marines in 1924. It has been placed above a collection of signage letters made from different materials.

PAGE 34 A corkscrew in the shape of a sailor is ready for action.

PAGE 35 Two clear glass, sailor-shaped liqueur bottles mingle with a collection of pitchers.

PAGES 36, 37, 38–39 A selection of works representing sailors in Rozensztroch's bedroom includes two original lithographs by the Greek painter Yannis Tsarouchis, a sailor holding his cap and another reclining on a sofa, *bottom left*. A painting by the Indian artist Sumatra Mukherjee hangs above a laughing Popeye figurine.

PAGES 40, 41 This rag doll, created by the French fashion designer Jean-Paul Gaultier and sold at auction for the benefit of the *Fondation Merci*, has found a home in an American Tramp Art frame.

PAGE 42 A vintage photograph of a sailor is the main element in a folk-art frame made from sculpted pieces of wood and a series of French patriotic symbols, which all reflect a seafaring theme.

PAGES 43, 44, 45 Enamel pins from the 1950s representing sailors are fixed onto Napoleon III-style cut-out metal frames that display symbols of the navy.

PAGES 46, 47 Two vintage photographs of anonymous sailors are a throwback to earlier times.

PAGES 48, 49 In the old days, the families of sailors deposited these silver ex-votos in their churches to protect their husbands and sons.

PAGES 50–51 In the South of France, there is an ancient tradition of crafting small figurines in terra cotta called *santons*, which mirror the daily life of the villagers.

PAGES 52–59 Numerous collectors from all generations love these small lead soldiers, of which there are many examples, including sailors, of course.

PAGES 60, 61 Many objects representing sailors were sold in the bazaars of port cities, like this napkin holder and two piggy banks in cast iron.

PAGES 62, 63 These vintage silk bandanas are decorated with a vocabulary specific to the navy.

35

45

52

THE CUTE LITTLE SAILOR

From an early age, children were dressed in sailor suits and given sailor-themed toys, with professional photographers as well as proud parents taking countless pictures of them. This innocent image was picked up by toy manufacturers and publishers of children's books. Sailors are depicted in figurines fashioned in a variety of materials and diverse attitudes, such as fishing, or playing a musical instrument. These objects have been made since the late 19th century, especially from the 1930s to the 1950s. Some call to mind Captain Archibald Haddock of Tintin fame, while a feminine figure emerges very occasionally from this masculine milieu.

OPPOSITE A rubber sailor seems to be in conversation with a happy baby.

PAGES 66–67, 68, 69 These sepia photographs showing children in sailor costumes include some who are sulking, while another, who is smiling, is dressed in a summer outfit and ready to put his small sailboat in the water in a public park. They contrast with the black-and-white image of a very serious child who, dressed in sailor garb, is celebrating his First Communion.

PAGES 70, 71, 72, 73 All kinds of vintage toys in wood and papier-mâché illustrate sailors in different stances—whether naive, realistic, or humorous.

PAGE 74 The British-born Beatrice Mallet, née Fox, was an illustrator for many children's books, as well as advertisements for Petit Bateau, a French clothing brand, from which the image on this postcard probably derives.

PAGES 75–77 On the cover of a 1950s book by the English writer Enid Blyton, Noddy obviously can't wait to be called out to sea!

PAGE 78 This girlishly plump and fair bisque porcelain figurine from the Napoleon III era has a matte, unglazed surface. The fragile toy must have belonged to a careful child, as witnessed by its well-preserved state.

PAGE 79 A 1930s celluloid baby rattle has also emerged unscathed after decades of use.

PAGES 80–85 The only thing missing from a series of rubber squeeze toys are the *squeak squeak* sounds they make.

PAGES 86, 87 Once upon a time, collecting pins and buttons was a popular hobby. These small ones are made from enamelled metal.

PAGES 88–92 Sailors transformed into dolls have been dressed in fabric suits and perform everyday tasks, related or not to their chores at sea.

PAGE 93 A small, painted plaster figurine finds its place among a collection of sailor-shaped toys.

PAGES 94–95 Look-alikes of Captain Archibald Haddock—Tintin's loyal companion—were cast in resin in a range of sizes.

PAGES 96–97, 98, 99 Elaborately carved wooden toys were produced in the Jura area of eastern France by specialized artisans. The four-wheeled boat would feel more at home on land than at sea.

91, Rue Lacourbe
(PAVILLON PARTICULIER)
Paris (XVe)

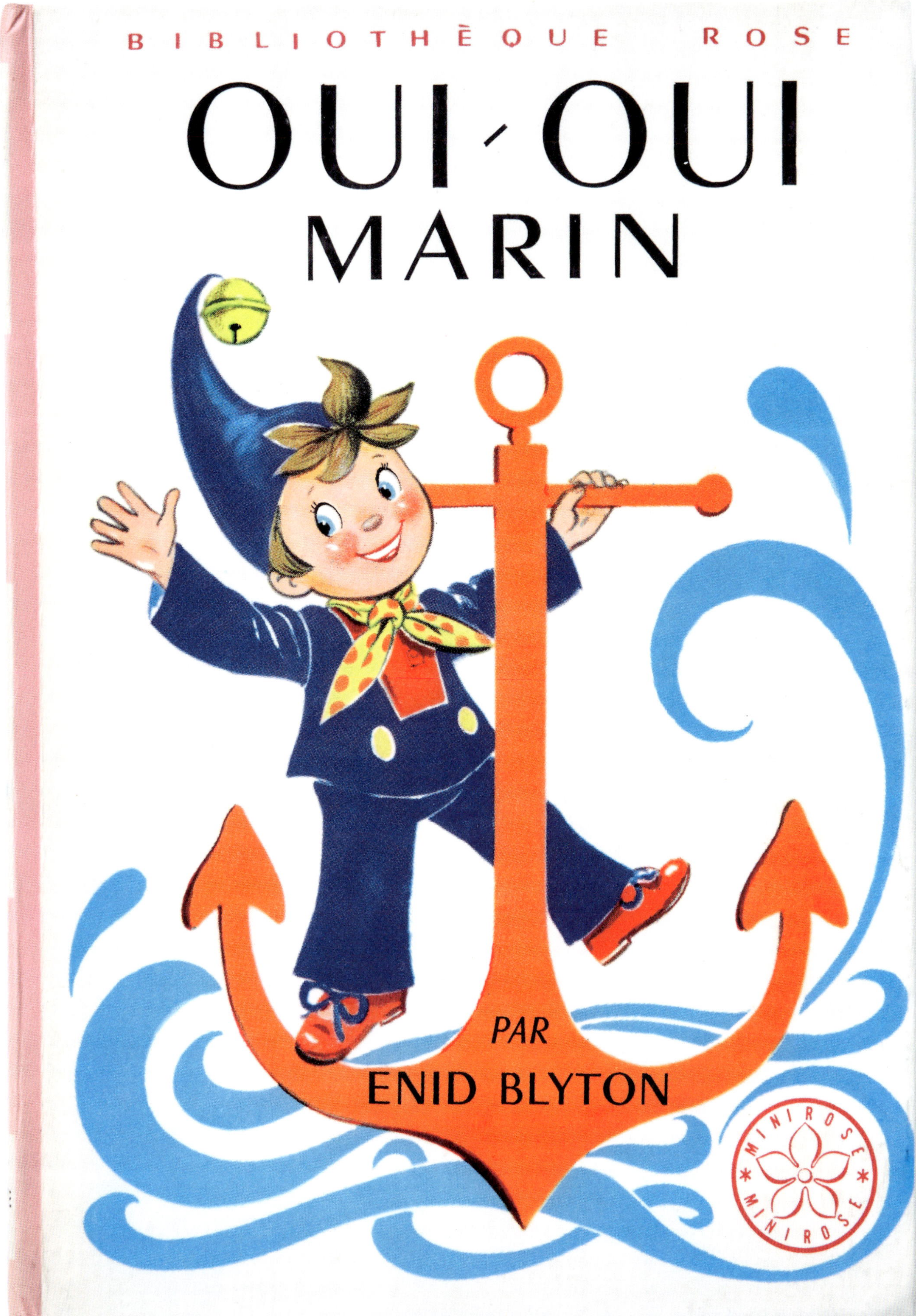
BIBLIOTHÈQUE ROSE
OUI-OUI
MARIN
PAR
ENID BLYTON
MINIROSE
MINIROSE

Écoute ! Elle klaxonne. Elle appelle au secours. »

« Tut ! Tut ! » L'auto dansait sur les vagues. « Tut ! Tut ! »

Heureusement, elle ne risquait pas de couler, car elle était presque toute en bois. Elle n'avait quand même pas l'air à son aise !

Deux marins qui l'avaient entendue accoururent.

« Une voiture ! s'exclama l'un d'eux. Elle est à toi, bonhomme en bois ? Ma parole ! C'est un chien qui nage vers elle !

L'auto dansait sur les vagues.

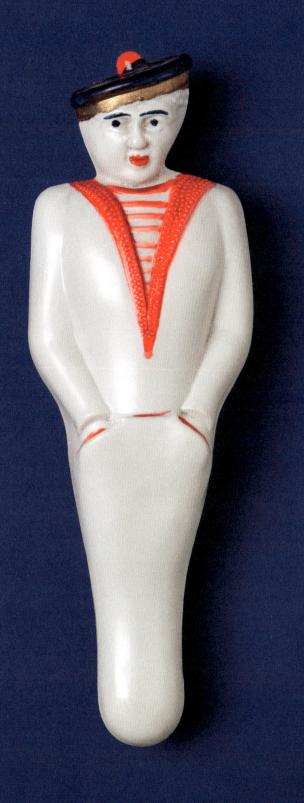

99

T'embrasser

*Oh! ma chérie, viens à mon secours,
J'ai soif de tes lèvres, j'ai soif de ton amour*

A sailor, by definition, is a man who goes far away to sea for long stretches of time, facing the hazards his job entails. He leaves his lovely sweetheart in one port or another, hoping she will faithfully await his return. To assure she will, he showers her with kitschy, romantic postcards brimming with stereotypical sentimental prose—of which a trove of folk imagery on the theme of the amorous sailor remains.

OPPOSITE Collecting postcards is an addictive hobby. This one represents a rather chaste kiss in the tradition of the movies of the 1930s and 1940s, but the sailor's prettily manicured nails give his ardor an added note of eloquence.

PAGES 102–106 With their naive charm, these have not escaped our author's keen eye. The sailor pining for his fiancée sends her postcards with corny, loving messages about how much he misses her.

PAGE 107 The theme is international. This German card illustrates the sailor's dream of coming home to his sweetheart for Christmas.

PAGE 108 In contrast to the previous cards, this one is quite explicit—the lady is scantily dressed, to the delight of her beau.

PAGE 109 In the 1950s, *Nous Deux* was a very popular magazine with young women dreaming of their Prince Charming. On this cover, he takes on a typical look of the era in the form of a curly-haired, handsome sailor—surely the hero of a photographic romance novel, which was a specialty of this publication. The slogan, "the weekly that brings happiness," alludes perhaps to the red pompom that his pretty companion might have touched.

THE SAILOR IN LOVE

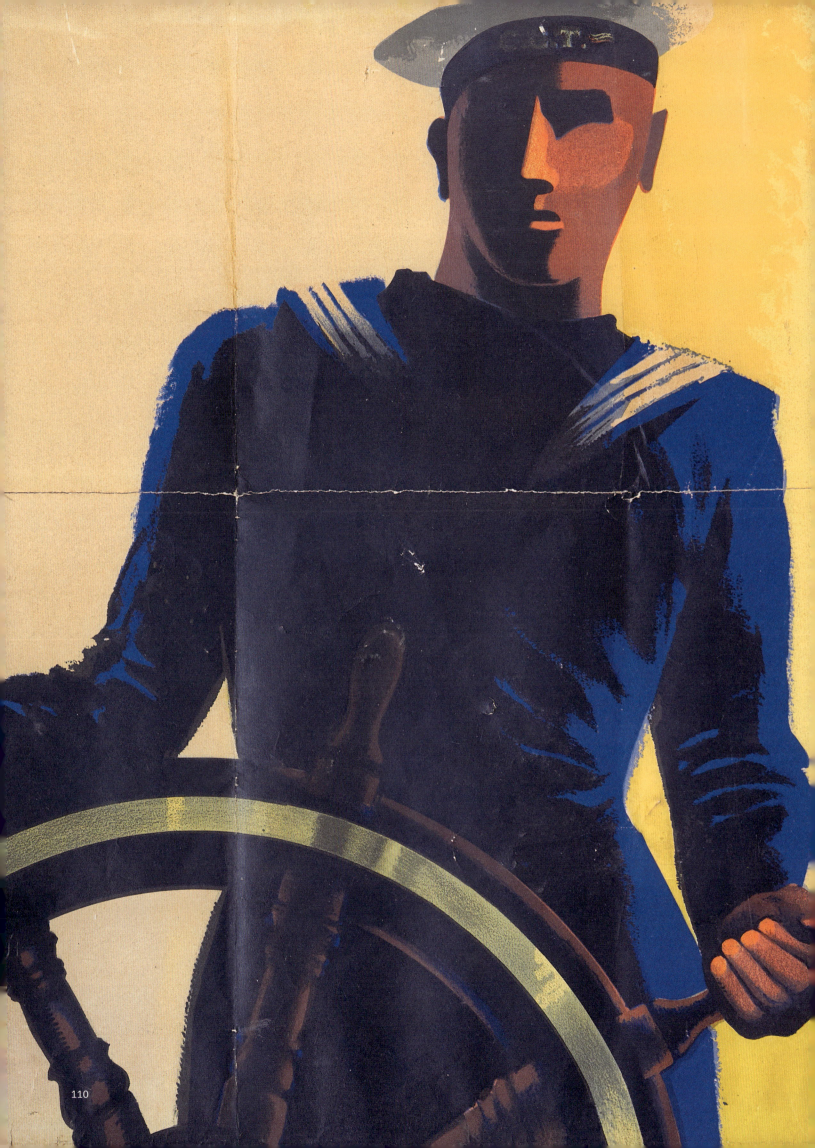

Different aspects of life on board are shown in this chapter. The sailor's uniform is the star, as well as all it takes to keep it and the ship in tip-top shape. Downtimes are productive, not only when the sailor is at ease but also when he has the time to write home and to wash and shave. He also plays cards with his companions and gets tattooed—a sure sign of bravery and manliness before stepping ashore on far-flung stopovers that are often punctuated with all sorts of amorous encounters, illustrated stereotypically when it comes to French sailors.

OPPOSITE A detail from a 1930s poster portrays a handsome sailor at the helm, drawn in the style of the period.

PAGES 112–113 The French word for seaman, *matelot*, derives from a Dutch expression meaning "bedfellow." Space was in short supply on 17th and 18th century ships, and crewmen were so tightly packed in together that they often had to share a hammock. Whether they used the hammocks in shifts or together is entirely up to your imagination.

PAGES 114–115, 116 Rubber stamps representing smiling sailors were often chosen to decorate their mailing envelopes.

PAGE 117 The iconic double-breasted pea jacket, made from waterproof wool broadcloth, is worn by sailors in cold weather. It was adopted by the British Royal Navy as early as 1800, and has since inspired countless designers and artists. The elegant jacket bestows a certain prestige on its wearer, and this sailor seems proud to have his picture taken wearing it.

PAGES 118–119 The legendary tattooed sailor is universal. This art was often practiced aboard ship by sailors who were amateur artists.

PAGES 120–127 Charles Millot, known as Henri Gervèse (1880–1959), a French painter and illustrator, was also a naval officer. We owe him this series of prints that amusingly depicts various facets of everyday life on board, and the way sailors worked around their limitations.

PAGES 128–129 A Thanksgiving card, written to a Polish-American, humorously reflects on the religious aspect of this holiday. Both the seaman and pilgrim kneel before a spread-tailed bird, while the dated stamp notes "Turkey Day." The anchors at the foot of the drawing and the naval stamp attest to the provenance of the card.

PAGES 130–131 Dated 1941, this cartoon on a postcard represents a sailor or officer boasting of his single-handed sinking of a submarine to a young recruit. It was sent from a United States Navy ship, as seen by the postage and date stamps.

PAGES 132–133 French composer Georges Auric created the music for the Russian writer and ballet librettist Boris Kochno's two-act, five-tableau ballet, which premiered in Paris in the Russian impresario Sergei Diaghilev's "Ballets Russes" in 1925. The production was certainly shown in Monaco the next year and memorialized by this postage stamp.

PAGES 134, 135 Two postcards illustrate sailors engaged in naughty activities while on stopovers in foreign lands.

THE SAILOR AT WORK AT SEA

Vie du Marin. Un hamac.

MARINS

quart de vin

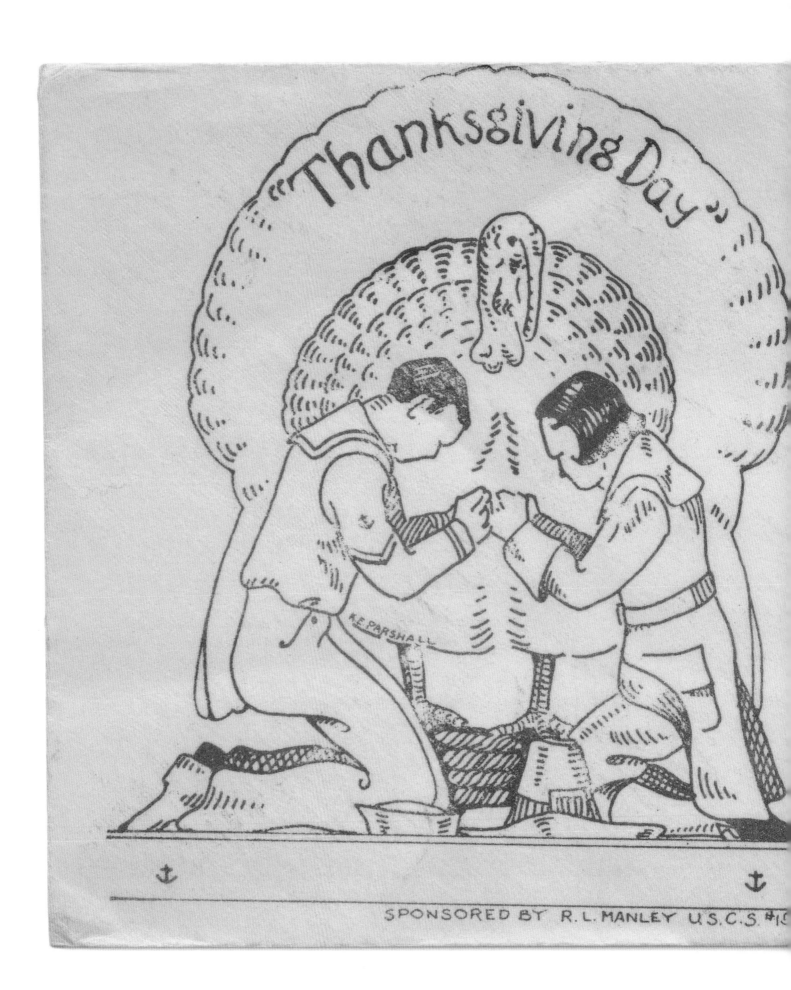

Mr. Eric Diem
719 Eighty Third St.
North Bergen, N. J.

1509 NOS MARINS (l'escale au Japon).

Une tasse de thé avec la mousmée.

1515 NOS MARINS (l'escale à Alger).

Causerie sous les palmiers.

Downtimes aboard ship gave free rein to the musical talents of some sailors. Compact instruments were preferred, and the popular accordion was a favorite. Musical scores, with their often smutty and, at times, questionable lyrics, illustrate the importance of song and music in the life of sailors of all nationalities. Sailor songs are part of a popular culture that went beyond the different ports from which they sailed.

THE SAILOR AS MUSICIAN

OPPOSITE, PAGE 138, AND 139 These three amazing objects are in fact liqueur bottles. The heads are corks, and the bases are ceramic music boxes. The sailor twirls to popular tunes when the mechanism is wound.

PAGE 140 An Art Deco-style ceramic accordion player was made in a type of popular earthenware that was very much in fashion as a decorative element in middle-class interiors in the 1930s. Pieces like this often represented people as well as animal figures, and were mass-produced in an off-white shade by companies such as Sarreguemines and Lunéville.

PAGE 141 A sailor playing the accordion is featured on this small ceramic, heart-shaped vase that dates from the 1950s.

PAGES 142–143 In the hands of a proud sailor, the accordion takes on a patriotic power as seen on this vintage Russian postcard.

PAGES 144–147 A portfolio from the 1930s assembles illustrated sheet music with famous sailor songs. The words of the songs, with their double meanings, seem as innocent as the illustrations, yet some are still very saucy!

PAGES 148–149 This song seems at face value as innocent as its illustrations, but the lyrics are, in fact, filled with racy double meanings!

2.
J'leur ai envoyé mon chat gris.(Bis)
Il leur fit voir la comédie.
  Jean du p'tit coq... etc.

3.
Ça m'fait penser à ma jolie (Bis)
Que dans pareil grenier je vis...
  Jean du p'tit coq... etc.

4.
J'y ai montré ma p'tite souris (Bis)
Et son p'tit chat l'a z'engloutie
  Jean du p'tit coq... etc.

5.
Quand il eut tout mangé è'm'dit: (Bis)
„Il mang'rait ben encore un p'tit".
  Jean du p'tit coq... etc.

6.
„C'est un vrai gourmand que j'lui dis (Bis)
„Poursûr qu'il aura l'premier prix!"
  Jean du p'tit coq... etc.

7.
„Pour si bien manger des souris (Bis)
„Fut-il à l'école de Paris?"
  Jean du p'tit coq... etc.

8.
→ „Y n'a jamais quitté l'pays!(Bis)..
.. Mon p'tit doigt lui a tout appris".
  Jean du p'tit coq... etc.

150

His look, uniform, and physical fitness make the sailor an ideal subject for his shipmates as well as many other artists, who all portray him with remarkable talent. Amateur artists, using any materials they had on hand, on board, or ashore, have created a unique maritime style featuring the sailor's most memorable attributes—the stripes, the hat, and his often macho pose.

OPPOSITE This sexy-looking, 10½-inch tall American sailor in a typical uniform was carved out of wood by an anonymous artist in the 1950s.

PAGES 152–153 A ceramic plaque portrays a sailor in his characteristic attire. The one-off ceramic piece was created for Rozensztroch by Gérard Durand, a fashion designer who, in his spare time, is an enthusiastic potter and artist. It evokes the title character from *Querelle de Brest*.

PAGES 154, 155 Is it a toy or a decorative object? In any case, it is a refreshingly innocent take on the sailor—shown in the back and front views of this painted earthenware figurine.

PAGES 156–157 Folk art is reflected in these two roughly fashioned and painted wooden bearded seamen. The color of their clothes is, however, uncharacteristic.

PAGES 158, 159 Dating from the late 19th century, this patriotic weathervane made of painted wood and metal is another example of folk art.

THE SAILOR AS ARTIST AND MODEL

159

Many cartoon and comic book characters are often dressed as sailors, no doubt to make them look friendly, even if rather gruesome at first glance. Their creators meant to spread a popular culture through these sailors whose nationalities have not the slightest importance as their images have become instantly identifiable.

THE CELEBRITY SAILOR

OPPOSITE Donald Duck, Walt Disney's famous character, made his first appearance in the movies in 1934 wearing a sailor costume. From then on, he became an international celebrity and took on myriad shapes, including that of this toy.

PAGES 162, 163 The Playmobil Ghostbusters Stay-Puft Marshmallow Man resembles a sailor-suited Michelin Man, the French tire character. In the 1984 *Ghostbusters* movie, the apparently jovial character is in fact a terrifying monster.

PAGE 164 At the height of the pin-collecting craze, this enamelled metal Popeye must have been quite a find.

PAGES 165, 166, 167 A grumpy Popeye confronts his archenemy and rival, Brutus, in a dispute over his sweetheart, Olive Oyl. The burly pirate, a sailor, too, has the upper hand until Popeye can get to his spinach. The image of Popeye the Sailor Man has been used time and time again in advertising.

Numerous everyday objects representing sailors and seamen have been produced all over the world—pipes, corkscrews, china. They evoke, often humorously, the life and work of those who left their families behind for months on end and did what they could to not be forgotten. Some of these objects were made by the sailors themselves, others were mass-produced to be sold in seaport gift and souvenir shops.

THE SAILOR AT HOME

OPPOSITE Pipe dream? Actually, a dream of a pipe. Or did the puffing sailor get smoke in his eyes?

PAGE 170 In America, the cookie jar was ubiquitous and existed in a very wide variety of shapes and sizes. Every house had one. This plump ceramic sailor from the 1950s is an example of one that is the envy of many collectors today.

PAGES 171, 172, 173 Sailor corkscrews in plastic and wood lend themselves perfectly to their given function.

PAGES 174, 175 In Italy, at the beginning of the 20th century, a wide variety of liqueurs were on the market and sold in molded glass bottles, which represented figures of all kinds, including sailors.

PAGES 176, 177 Vintage American drinking glasses are decorated with sailors dancing exuberantly.

PAGE 178 "Today's Special" is illustrated on an Italian plate that came from a restaurant in Genoa, Italy. If you ordered the dish, you could take the plate home with you.

PAGE 179 The French artist Gérard Durand made this stylized sailor-themed plate and spoon especially for this book as a gift to its author.

172

Le matelot Gérard, 18 ans, un des premiers décorés de la médaille militaire et de la croix de guerre 1939 pour acte de bravoure en mer. (16.307.)

L'HEBDOMADAIRE DE L'ACTUALITÉ MONDIALE 9 NOVEMBRE 1939

Stamp collecting is the mother of all collections. This nautical-themed one has found its natural place here. The sailor has, in fact, been seen as a hero throughout the ages, accomplishing great feats. Whether officers or crewmen, sailors went down with their ships, and were celebrated posthumously. How better to do this than with a commemorative postage stamp? Stamps travel and carry with them the images of these heroes, who are consecrated at last by a grateful nation. As this chapter illustrates, many seamen proved their valor through the conflicts of the last century, regardless of nationality or their rank aboard ship.

OPPOSITE This 18-year-old sailor, one of the first to be awarded a *Croix de Guerre*, a military medal for an act of bravery at sea, was celebrated on the cover of the weekly French magazine *Match* in 1939.

PAGES 182-183 This envelope was mailed on January 3, 1948, from the USS Massey, a United States Navy destroyer that served between 1944 and 1973.

PAGES 184-185 World War II sailors were depicted as heroes on a 1945 American postage stamp.

PAGES 186-189 A First Day Issue envelope commemorates four distinguished sailors and naval officers. Included is Doris Miller (1919-1943), the first African American to be awarded the Navy Cross for his bravery during the attack on Pearl Harbor on December 7, 1941. He perished in November 1943, when an enemy submarine torpedoed the aircraft carrier on which he was serving.

PAGES 190-191 This 1946, 3-cent stamp commemorates refueling, an essential aspect of the United States Navy during and after World War II. Here a United States Merchant Marine ship is loading or unloading its cargo.

PAGES 192, 193 Both South Africa and the Soviet Union celebrated the sailor on their postage stamps during and after World War II.

PAGES 194-197 In 1967, the German Democratic Republic (GDR), known as East Germany, celebrated the 50th anniversary of the Communist Revolution with a particular emphasis on its sailors. They are represented in a group on a stamp where a splash of red needs no explaination.

PAGES 198-199 With this stamp, the French Postal Service commemorated the memory of this helicopter aircraft carrier, *Jeanne d'Arc*, which was built in the arsenal of Brest, in Brittany, from 1959 to 1961, and was retired from service in June of 2010.

THE HEROIC SAILOR

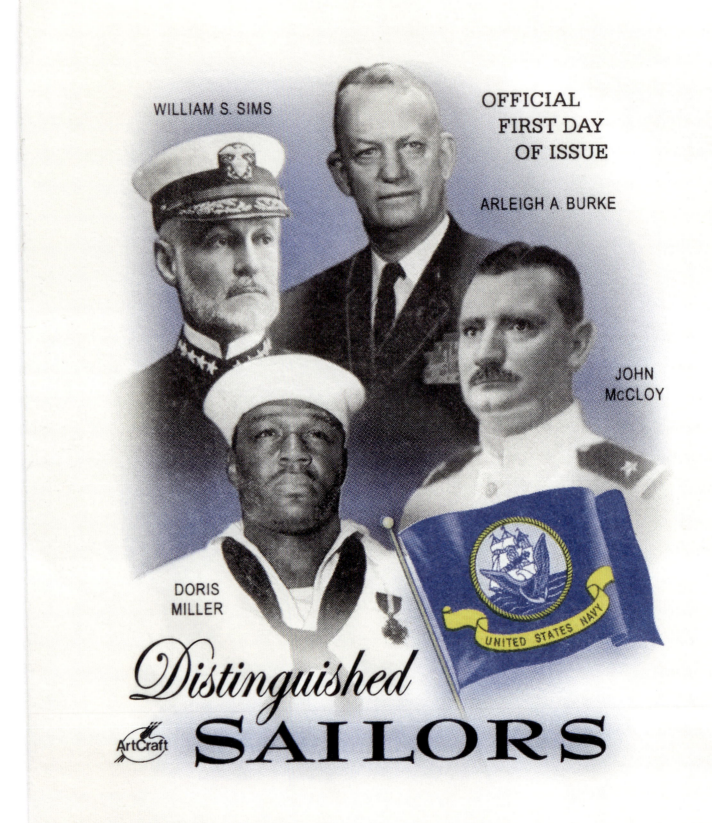

The erotic studio photographs that precede the very daring illustrations from *Querelle de Brest*, by Jean Genet, attest to the powerful fantasies surrounding the sailor, a quintessential target of lust. A single vintage pin-up girl by the famous Peruvian-born artist Alberto Vargas emerges from a sea of men. In every one of these images, a symbolic token of the sailor's uniform or his environment—a fishing net, ropes, or a bollard—sets the scene and serves to compose the erotic showcase for the sailor's naked or partially clothed body. A supremely virile and toned body is unambiguously displayed as an object of desire. Were these images clandestinely distributed? Who knows?

THE SEXY SAILOR

OPPOSITE, 202-212 These erotic photographs of sailors were all taken in a studio during the 1960s.

PAGE 213 A color illustration of a scantily clad sailor shining his crewmate's shoes stands out from all the black-and-white illustrations.

PAGES 214-215 Alberto Vargas is most notably known for his drawings of pin-up girls from the 1940s. Sailors adored them and used them to decorate the insides of their lockers.

PAGES 216-229 The French poet and artist Jean Cocteau fell under the spell of Jean Genet (1910-1986), a writer with a shady reputation and ambiguous political views. Cocteau illustrated this volume, titled *Querelle de Brest*. Published in 1947 with a modest numbered print run of 460 copies, it was distributed in secret. It included 29 of Cocteau's homoerotic full-page lithographs, of which some are shown here. It is noteworthy that this opus wasn't published by Gallimard in its first prestigious La Pléiade edition of the collected works of Jean Genet. This has since been remedied.

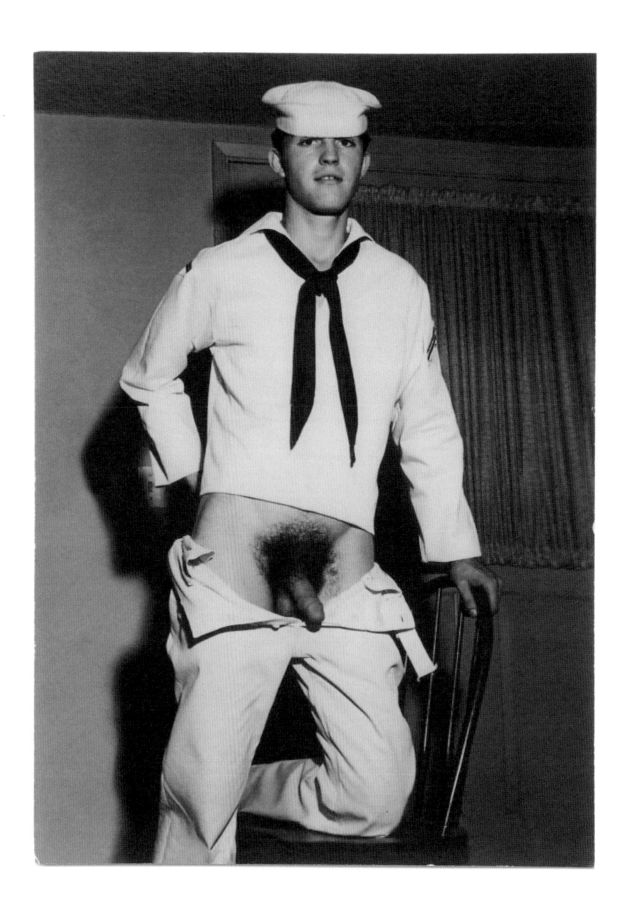

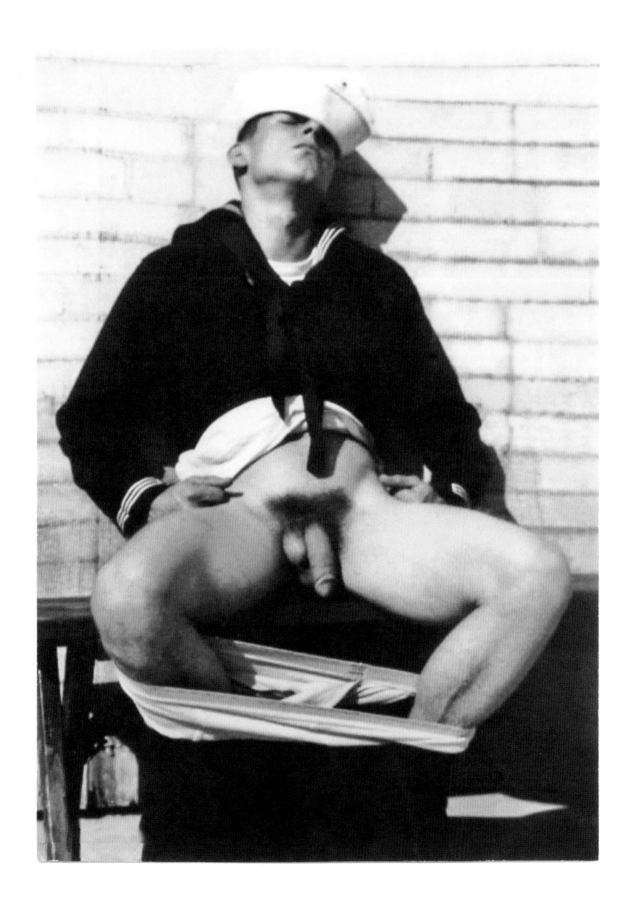

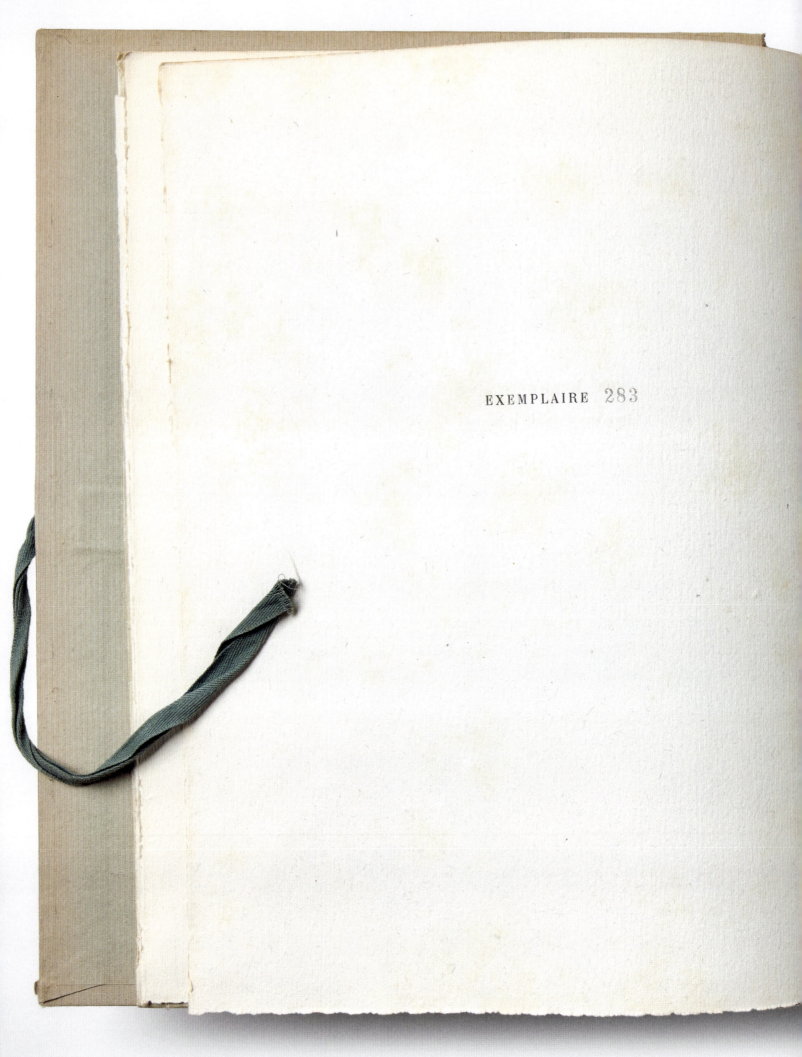
EXEMPLAIRE 283

JEAN GENET

QUERELLE
DE
BREST

**QUERELLE
DE BREST**

QUERELLE DE BREST

chaque instant. Il ignore le rêve. Sa présence est éternelle. Il ne répond jamais, « l'esprit comme ailleurs. » Et pourtant la puérilité de ses préoccupations apparentes me déroute.

Les mains dans les poches de mon pantalon, flemmard, je lui dirais :

« Bouscule-moi un peu pour faire tomber la cendre de ma cigarette. » Et vachement, en homme, Il me tirerait un coup de poing dans l'épaule. Je m'ébroue. »

J'aurais pu rester droit, m'accrocher à la rembarde, le roulis n'était pas si grand, mais je profitai promptement, avec joie, du mouvement du bateau pour me laisser déporter, osciller, et chaque fois dans sa direction. Je réussis même à frôler son coude.

Un molosse cruel et dévoué à son maître, prêt à vous dévorer la carotide, semblait le suivre, et parfois marcher entre ses mollets, les flancs de la bête se confondant avec les muscles des cuisses prêt à mordre, grondant toujours et montrant les crocs, et si féroce qu'on s'attendait à le voir arracher les couilles à Querelle.

Après ces quelques notes relevées çà et là, mais non au hasard, dans un carnet intime qui nous le suggère, nous désirons qu'il vous apparaisse que le matelot Querelle, né de cette solitude où l'officier lui-même restait reclus, était un personnage solitaire comparable à l'ange de l'Apocalypse dont les pieds reposent sur la mer. A force de méditer de Querelle, d'user par l'imagination ses plus beaux ornements, ses muscles, ses bosses, ses dents, son sexe deviné, pour le lieutenant Seblon le matelot est devenu un ange (il écrira, nous le verrons plus loin, « l'ange de la solitude ») c'est-à-dire un être de plus en plus inhumain, cristallin, autour de qui se développent les bandes d'une musique basée sur le contraire de l'harmonie, ou plutôt une musique qui est ce qui demeure quand l'harmonie est usée, passée à la meule, au milieu de quoi cet ange immense se meut, lentement, sans témoin, les pieds sur l'eau, mais la tête — ou ce qui devrait être sa tête — dans la confusion des rayons d'un soleil surnaturel. Qu'afin de dérober à l'ennemi des plans précieux dont la connaissance nous sauvera, se prépare un agent secret, le but qu'il poursuit conserve si précisément notre destin, que nous sommes attachés, suspendus à sa réussite, et ce but s'en avère d'une telle noblesse qu'à la pensée de celui qui le réalisera, la poitrine se gonfle d'émotion, de nos yeux coulent des larmes, cependant que lui-même s'entraîne à sa tâche avec une froide méthode. Examinant les plus efficaces, il essaie des techniques, bref, il poursuit

16

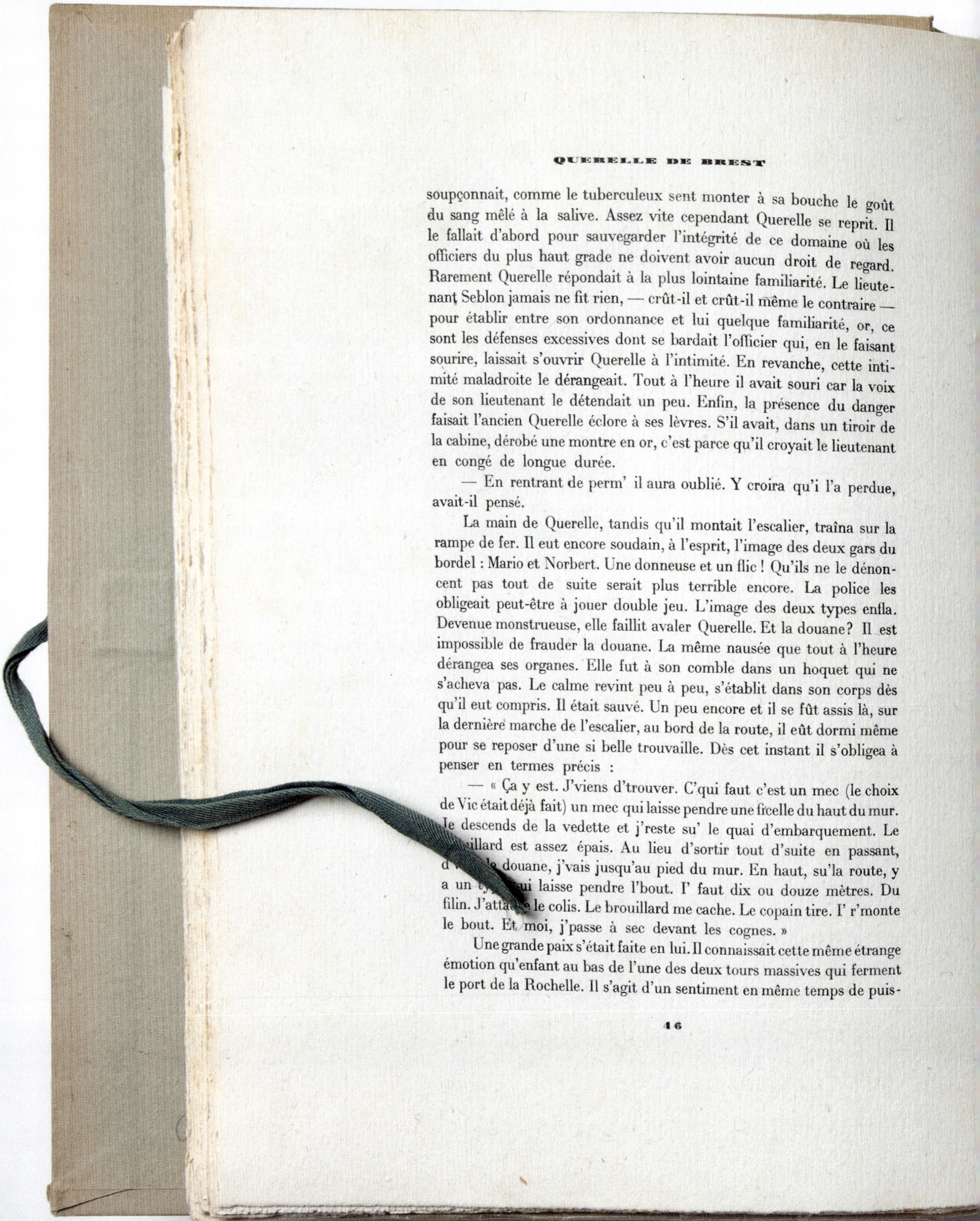

QUERELLE DE BREST

soupçonnait, comme le tuberculeux sent monter à sa bouche le goût du sang mêlé à la salive. Assez vite cependant Querelle se reprit. Il le fallait d'abord pour sauvegarder l'intégrité de ce domaine où les officiers du plus haut grade ne doivent avoir aucun droit de regard. Rarement Querelle répondait à la plus lointaine familiarité. Le lieutenant Seblon jamais ne fit rien, — crût-il et crût-il même le contraire — pour établir entre son ordonnance et lui quelque familiarité, or, ce sont les défenses excessives dont se bardait l'officier qui, en le faisant sourire, laissait s'ouvrir Querelle à l'intimité. En revanche, cette intimité maladroite le dérangeait. Tout à l'heure il avait souri car la voix de son lieutenant le détendait un peu. Enfin, la présence du danger faisait l'ancien Querelle éclore à ses lèvres. S'il avait, dans un tiroir de la cabine, dérobé une montre en or, c'est parce qu'il croyait le lieutenant en congé de longue durée.

— En rentrant de perm' il aura oublié. Y croira qu'i l'a perdue, avait-il pensé.

La main de Querelle, tandis qu'il montait l'escalier, traîna sur la rampe de fer. Il eut encore soudain, à l'esprit, l'image des deux gars du bordel : Mario et Norbert. Une donneuse et un flic ! Qu'ils ne le dénoncent pas tout de suite serait plus terrible encore. La police les obligeait peut-être à jouer double jeu. L'image des deux types enfla. Devenue monstrueuse, elle faillit avaler Querelle. Et la douane ? Il est impossible de frauder la douane. La même nausée que tout à l'heure dérangea ses organes. Elle fut à son comble dans un hoquet qui ne s'acheva pas. Le calme revint peu à peu, s'établit dans son corps dès qu'il eut compris. Il était sauvé. Un peu encore et il se fût assis là, sur la dernière marche de l'escalier, au bord de la route, il eût dormi même pour se reposer d'une si belle trouvaille. Dès cet instant il s'obligea à penser en termes précis :

— « Ça y est. J'viens d'trouver. C'qui faut c'est un mec (le choix de Vic était déjà fait) un mec qui laisse pendre une ficelle du haut du mur. J'descends de la vedette et j'reste su' le quai d'embarquement. Le brouillard est assez épais. Au lieu d'sortir tout d'suite en passant, d'vant la douane, j'vais jusqu'au pied du mur. En haut, su'la route, y a un type qui laisse pendre l'bout. I' faut dix ou douze mètres. Du filin. J'attache le colis. Le brouillard me cache. Le copain tire. I' r'monte le bout. Et moi, j'passe à sec devant les cognes. »

Une grande paix s'était faite en lui. Il connaissait cette même étrange émotion qu'enfant au bas de l'une des deux tours massives qui ferment le port de la Rochelle. Il s'agit d'un sentiment en même temps de puis-

46

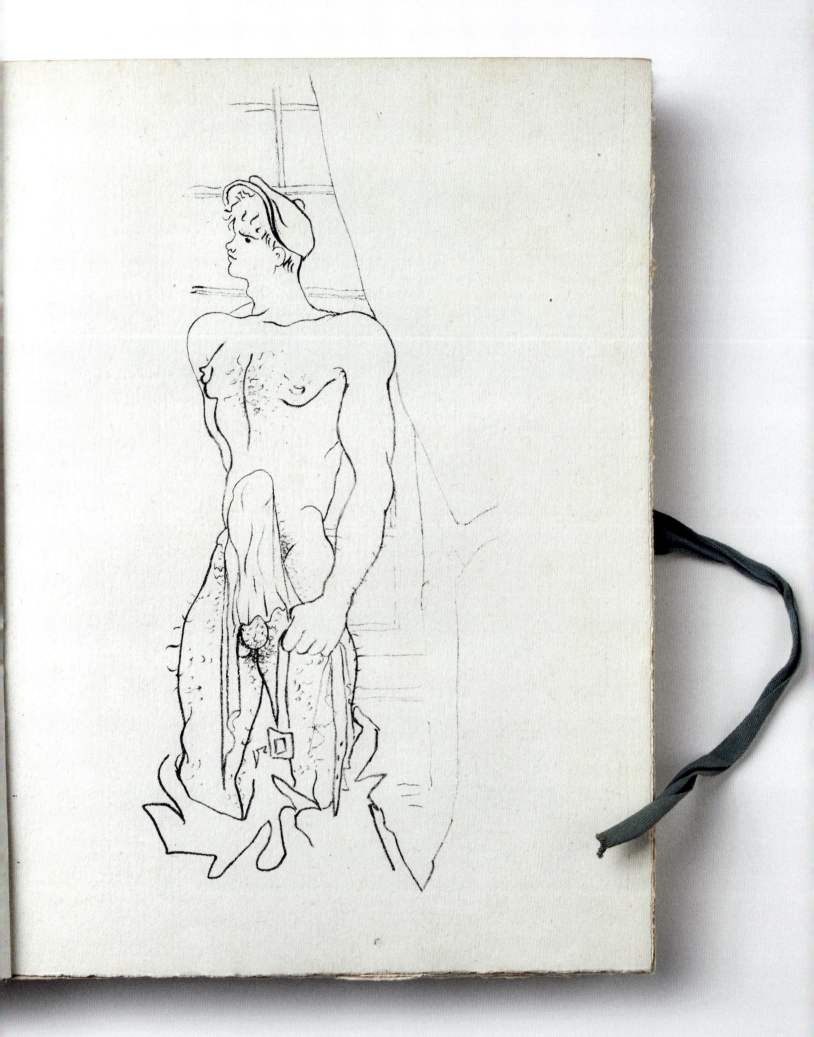

Cependant — et ceci ne paraît étrange qu'aux lecteurs qui n'auront pas éprouvés ces instants révélateurs — le policier chassa cette connaissance comme si elle eût été un danger pour lui-même. Il la surmonta. Il l'enterra sous l'épaisseur de sa réflexion. Le Lieutenant continuait sa comédie intérieure. Il la dépassait presque. Il était sûr maintenant de sa réussite. Il se liait au jeune maçon d'une façon de plus en plus mystique — et étroite — à mesure qu'il semblait s'écarter de lui, non seulement en niant son agression, mais en se défendant de le défendre par un souci de générosité. Niant sa générosité, le Lieutenant la détruisait en soi-même et ne laissait subsister qu'une indulgence à l'égard du criminel, et davantage encore une participation morale au crime. Cette culpabilité devait le trahir finalement. Le lieutenant Seblon insulta le commissaire. Il osa le gifler. Lui-même sentait que de méprisables cabotinages sont à l'origine des beautés graves qui font l'œuvre d'art. Il atteignait et dépassait Gil. Le même mécanisme qui avait permis au lieutenant Seblon de nier l'agression de Gil, l'avait fait autrefois se montrer lâche et bas à l'égard de Querelle.

« Vas-y Jules ! Crache ou j't'étrangle ! Combat de juifs. Cinq contre un. »

Cette dernière expression qu'il aimait signifiait parfaitement son attitude. Il était *fier* de ne rien craindre, de si bien être à l'abri de toutes les représailles dans son uniforme galonné. Cette lâcheté est une grande force. Or, il suffit d'une légère torsion pour qu'elle affrontât un autre ennemi, (très exactement, son contraire), pour qu'elle s'affrontât elle-même. S'il punissait ou vexait Querelle sans raison, nous disons que l'officier était lâche. Mais au centre de son acte il connaissait la présence d'une volonté ou force — sa force — : c'est elle qui lui permettra de quitter le dîner sans avoir parlé, c'est cette force encore (découverte et cultivée au centre de sa lâcheté) qui lui permettra d'insulter le policier. Enfin, emporté par son souffle généreux, soutenu par la présence lumineuse du vrai coupable, il s'accusa lui-même du vol de l'argent. Lorsqu'il entendit le commissaire donner l'ordre aux inspecteurs de l'arrêter, Seblon fit secrètement appel à son prestige d'officier de marine, mais lorsqu'il fut bouclé dans une des cellules du poste, certain que le scandale serait terrible à bord, il fut heureux.

police songea qu'un pédéraste en était peut-être l'auteur. Quand on sait avec quelle horreur la société écarte d'elle toute idée qui la rapproche de l'idée de pédérastie, il faudrait s'étonner que la police acceptât si facilement d'y recourir. Or si, un crime accompli, la police propose d'abord ouvertement ce mobile : intérêt d'argent ou drame passionnel, quand l'un des acteurs est ou fut un matelot, tout simplement elle songe : perversion sexuelle. Elle s'empare de cette idée avec une précipitation presque douloureuse. A la société la police est ce qu'est le rêve à l'activité quotidienne ; ce qu'elle s'interdit à soi-même, dès qu'elle le peut, la société polie autorise la police à l'évoquer. De là peut-être vient le sentiment de dégoût et d'attirance mêlés qu'on a à son égard. Chargée de drainer les rêves, la police les retient dans ses filtres. Ainsi expliquerons-nous que les policiers ressemblent tant à ceux qu'ils chassent. Car il serait faux de croire que c'est pour mieux le tromper, le dépister et le vaincre, que les inspecteurs se confondent si bien avec leur gibier. En examinant attentivement le comportement intime de Mario, nous y trouverons d'abord sa fréquentation de bordel et son amitié avec le patron. Sans doute trouve-t-il en Norbert un indicateur qui est en quelque sorte un trait d'union entre la société avouable et une activité suspecte, mais encore il prend — s'il ne les avait, avec une étonnante facilité, les manières et l'argot des voyous — manières et langages qu'il exagère dans le danger. Enfin, sa volonté d'aimer d'une façon coupable Dédé nous est une indication : cet amour l'écarte de la police où l'on doit être d'une parfaite pureté. (Ces propositions sont apparemment des contradictions. Nous verrons comment celles-ci se résolvent dans les faits.) Gorgée de besognes dont nous refusons l'aveu, la police est maudite, et davantage la police secrète qui au centre (et protégée par eux) des uniformes bleus sombres des flics nous apparaît avec la délicatesse des poux translucides, petits joyaux fragiles, facilement écrasés par l'ongle, et dont le corps est bleu, de s'être nourri du bleu sombre d'un jersey. Cette malédiction lui offre de se livrer furieusement à ces besognes. Dès qu'elle en a l'occasion, la police se rue sur l'idée de pédérastie dont heureusement elle ne peut débrouiller le mystère. Confusément les inspecteurs comprirent que le meurtre d'un matelot près des remparts n'était pas dans l'ordre : on aurait dû découvrir une « tante » assassinée, abandonnée sur l'herbe et dépouillée de son argent et de ses bijoux. A sa place, on trouvait son assassin logique avec, dans ses poches, son argent. Cette anomalie, sans doute, troublait un peu les policiers, dérangeait le déroulement de leur pensée, sans pourtant les gêner

Querelle à son étoile accordera une confiance absolue. Cette étoile devait son existence à la confiance qu'avait en elle le matelot — elle était si l'on veut l'écrasement sur sa nuit du rayon de sa confiance en, justement, sa confiance, et pour que l'étoile conserve sa grandeur et son éclat, c'est-à-dire son efficacité, Querelle devait conserver sa confiance en elle — qui était sa confiance en soi — et d'abord son sourire afin que le plus subtil nuage ne s'interposât entre l'étoile et lui, afin que le rayon ne diminuât d'énergie, afin que le doute le plus vaporeux ne fît l'étoile se ternir un peu. Il restait suspendu à elle née à chaque seconde de lui. Or elle le protégeait effectivement. La crainte de la voir soufflée créait en lui une sorte de vertige. Querelle vivait à toute allure. Son attention tendue pour nourrir toujours son étoile, l'obligeait à une précision de mouvements qu'une vie molle n'eût pas obtenue de lui (car à quoi bon?). Toujours sur le qui-vive il voyait mieux l'obstacle et quel geste hardiment faire pour l'éviter. C'est seulement quand il sera épuisé (s'il l'est jamais) qu'il flanchera. Sa certitude de posséder une étoile venait d'un entrelacs de circonstances (que nous appelons un bonheur) assez hasardeux encore qu'organisé, et de telle sorte, puisque c'est en rosaces — qu'on est tenté d'y rechercher une raison métaphysique. Bien avant que d'entrer dans les Equipages de la Flotte, Querelle avait entendu la chanson intitulée « l'Etoile d'Amour ».

> « *Tous les marins ont une étoile*
> *Qui les protège dans les cieux.*
> *Quand à leurs yeux rien ne la voile*
> *Le malheur ne peut rien contre eux* ».

Les soirs d'ivresse, les dockers la faisaient chanter à l'un des leurs qui gueulait bien. Le gars se laissait d'abord prier, servir à boire, enfin il se levait et, au milieu des costauds appuyés sur la table, pour les enchanter, sortaient de sa bouche édentée des paroles de rêve :

> « *C'est vous Nina que j'ai choisie*
> *Parmi tous les astres du soir*
> *Et vous êtes sans le savoir*
> *L'Etoile de ma vie...* »

A big thank you goes to all of you who have helped me realize *Ahoy Sailor!*

Francis Amiand, Christophe Anjolras, Julian Cosma, Françoise Dorget, Adrienne Dubessay, Arnaud Dubessay, Gérard Durand, Frederico Farina, Cathie Fidler, Gianluca Gimini, Niki Gripari, Alexandre Jolivet, Laurence Leclerc, Jacques Lefebvre-Linetzky, Mark London, Davide Mariani, Martine Marescaux, Marie-Pierre Morel, Paola Navone, Gennaro Nobile, Alexis de Prevoisin, Christine Puech, Paula Rubenstein, Shiri Slavin, Suzanne Slesin, Dominique Tosiani, Yani Tzimas, and Dyllia Zannettos.
—Daniel Rozensztroch, Paris, November, 2023

INDEX

Art Deco, 137
Art Nouveau, 25
Auric, Georges, 111

Babcock, Richard Fayerweather, 232
Bakelite, 20
Blyth, Ann, 232
Blyton, Enid, 65
Brest, France, 181
British Royal Navy, 111

Cannes, France, 19
Christy, Howard Chandler, 232
Cocteau, Jean, 20, 201

Dadaism, 20
Diaghilev, Sergei, 111
Disney, Walt, 161
Donald Duck, 20, 161
Duplo, 20
Durand, Gérard, 151, 169, 231

Folk Art, 16, 25, 151
France, 16, 19, 20, 25, 111, 181
French Postal Service, 181
French Navy, 19, 111
   Jeanne d'Arc, 181
Fondation Merci, Paris, 25

Gallimard, 201
   La Pléiade, 201
Gaultier, Jean-Paul, 19, 25, 232
   "Boy Toy" collection, 19
Genet, Jean, 20, 201
   Querelle de Brest, 20, 151, 201
Genoa, Italy, 169
German Democratic Republic, (GDR), 181, 232
Ghostbusters, 161

Jorgensen, Victor, 232
Jura, France, 65

Kochno, Boris, 111

Lunéville, France 137

Mallet, Beatrice, 65
Marseille, France, 25
Match, 181
Mediterranean Sea, 19
Michelin Man, 161
Miller, Doris, 181
Millot, Charles, 111
Monaco, 111
Mukherjee, Sumatra, 25

Napoleon III, 65
Napoleon III-style, 25
Navy Cross, 181
Netherlands, 19
New York Times, 232
Nous Deux, 101

Outsider Art, 20

Paris, France, 111
Pearl Harbor, Hawaii, 181
Peck, Gregory, 232
Petit Bateau, 65
Playmobil, 20
   Ghostbusters Stay-Puft Marshmallow Man, 161
Popeye the Sailor Man, 20
   Brutus, 161
   Oyl, Olive, 161
   Popeye, the Sailor Man, 25, 161

Radiguet, 20
Remi, Georges (Hergé), 20
   Tintin, 20, 65
   Haddock, Captain Archibald, 20, 65
Romania, 19

Saint-Jean-de-Luz, France, 232
Sarreguemines, France, 137
Scheveningen, Netherlands, 19
South Africa, 181
Soviet Union, 181

The Hague, Netherlands, 19
The World in His Arms, 232
Tramp Art, 19, 25
Tsarouchis, Yannis, 20, 25
   The Forgotten Guard, 20

United Kingdom, 19
United States (America), 19, 111, 151, 169, 181, 232
United States Merchant Marine, 181
United States Navy, 19, 111, 181, 232
   Sixth Fleet, 19
   USS Belle Grove, 232
   USS Massey, 181

Vargas, Alberto, 201
Vertury, George de, 25
Virgin Mary, 25

World War II, 181, 232

COVER AND BACK COVER The sexy-looking, 10½-inch tall American sailor in a typical uniform was carved out of wood by an anonymous artist in the 1950s.

ENDPAPERS The blue striped sailor t-shirt has become very popular, especially since the French fashion designer Jean-Paul Gaultier has made it his signature piece.

BACK OF FRONT ENDPAPERS Even ladies took up the theme of the sailor—a woman embroidered this doily in a stem stitch.

PAGES 2-3 All the sailors in the world wear with pride a sailor hat with the name of their ship.

OPPOSITE TITLE The sailor or navy officer was often the hero of many Hollywood movies, including 1952 *The World in His Arms*, a seafaring adventure starring Gregory Peck and Ann Blyth.

PAGES 6-7 In 1967, the The German Democratic Republic (DDR), known as East Germany, celebrated the 50th anniversary of the Communist Revolution with a particular emphasis on the sailor.

PAGE 8 This photograph by the United States Navy photojournalist Victor Jorgensen graced the front page of the *New York Times* on August 14, 1945. A sailor is shown passionately kissing a woman during the celebration that marked V-J Day, the end of World War II.

PAGES 10, 11 Sailors used to have their portraits—which now look quite old fashioned—taken in front of studio backdrops in the port cities they visited.

PAGES 12-13 A Christmas greeting, mailed from the USS Belle Grove in 1968, featured a sailor with his pal, Santa Claus.

PAGES 14, 15 These recruitment posters for the United States Navy were created at the beginning of the 20th century, aimed at young men and appealing to their virility. The one on the left, by the American artist Richard Fayerweather Babcock, was released in 1918; the one on the right, by the American artist Howard Chandler Christy—known for his "Christy Girls"—dates from 1917, the same year women could join the Navy.

PAGE 230 On the back of a postcard from the town of Saint-Jean-de-Luz, in the South of France, which the author found in a flea market, a line drawing portrays a profile of a sailor.

OPPOSITE To close, this very small sailor's hat meant for a doll was made in wool and topped with a red pompom for good luck.

Every effort has been made to locate copyright holders; any omissions will be corrected in future printings.
All photographs by Francis Amiand except for the following:
Page 8: Photograph by Lt. Victor Jorgensen/Navy. Page 14: Courtesy of Mark London, Pimlico Prints. Page 15: Courtesy of The University of Alabama Libraries Special Collections. Pages 36, 38–39: Courtesy © Yannis Tsarouchis Foundation. Page 180: (DR) Droit Reservé. Pages 217, 218, 221, 223, 225, 227, 229: ©2024 Artists Rights Society (ARS), New York / ADAGP, Paris.

DANIEL ROZENSZTROCH has been a longtime consultant for the magazine *Marie Claire Maison* and was the creative director of *Merci* in Paris, France. He is also the co-author of a series of titles in the Style Series (Clarkson Potter), as well as a number of books on the subject of everyday things, including *Wire* and *Kitchen Ceramics* (Abbeville Press); and *Herring: A Love Story, Spoon*, and *A Life of Things* (Pointed Leaf Press).

After teaching English as a foreign language in Nice, France, for many years, CATHIE FIDLER published three novels and three collections of short stories in French. One of them, *In Hazy Zones* (Edilivre), is available in English. She also co-authored *Herring: A Love Story* (Pointed Leaf Press), with Daniel Rozensztroch Her blog, *Gratitude*, (http://gratitude-leblogdecathiefidler.blogspot.fr) focuses on some of the more positive aspects of our world.

PUBLISHER Suzanne Slesin
CREATIVE DIRECTOR Frederico Farina
EDITORIAL ASSISTANT Julian Cosma
COPY EDITOR Anouck Dussaud

ISBN 978-1-938461-56-9
LIBRARY OF CONGRESS NUMBER 2023919282
FIRST EDITION
PRINTED IN SPAIN

Ahoy Sailor! © 2024 Daniel Rozensztroch. All rights reserved under international copyrights conventions. No part of this book, or any of its contents, may be reproduced, utilized, or transmitted in any form or by any means, electronic or mechanical, including photocopying, recording, or by any information storage and retrieval system, or otherwise, without permission in writing from the publisher. Please direct inquiries to info@pointedleafpress.com. Pointed Leaf Press, LLC. 136 Baxter Street, Suite 1C, New York, New York 10013.